# ORISA IBEJI

**DRAMA**

# Kraftgriots

*Also in the series* (DRAMA)

# ORISA IBEJI

**DRAMA**

Ahmed Yerima

*Published by*

**Kraft Books Limited**
6A Polytechnic Road, Sango, Ibadan
Box 22084, University of Ibadan Post Office
Ibadan, Oyo State, Nigeria
✆ +234803 348 2474, +234805 129 1191
E-mail: kraftbooks@yahoo.com
Website: www.kraftbookslimited.com

First published 2014

ISBN 978–978–918–190–2

= KRAFTGRIOTS =
(A literary imprint of Kraft Books Limited)

First printing, July 2014

# DEDICATION

For my remaining dear and loving friends, now few, lonely, and left behind in Zaria. God bless you all.

# AUTHOR'S NOTE

The month of February 2014, will remain a very sad month in my life. I lost three great friends: Jenkeri Okwori, Martins Ayegba, and Samuel Kafewo in one fell swoop. The first two I made in my teaching years at Ahmadu Bello University, Zaria; and the third, who arrived Zaria after I had left, became my dear friend through mutual respect for each other. As a result of this tragic occurrence, my state of mind made writing this new play tedious and sad. If I include Hadiza Ampa, Aderemi Bamikunle, and Yakubu Nasidi who had died earlier, it would then mean Death (*Iku*), in collaboration with Mother Earth (*Ile*), supervised by Esu (*Odara*) the Master of the place where three footpaths meet, would have taken six great pals from me in Zaria alone, But I remain resolute.

In this new play, *Orisa Ibeji,* the duality of the human persona, the symbolic essence of the effigy of the twin (*ibeji*) mythology among my chosen Yoruba people, and the supremacy of destiny are my thematic preoccupations. I shall let the play speak for itself as my heart remains heavily wrapped up in white shrouds, probably locked up in the caskets of my dear gone friends. Ummmhhh.

I thank my family, and Chief Yemi Adeyemi, as always.

**Ahmed Yerima**
*Ago-Iwoye, February, 2014.*

# DRAMATIS PERSONAE

Iya Olorisa
Adedigba
Olori Mojisola
Iyalode
Balogun
Otun
Oluawo
Jaguna
Ifadunbe
Saura
Akuda
Ilari
Iyun
Tade
Ikate
Yinyin
Bante
Ifajana
Iya
Abese
Abore
Madwoman
Adebimpe
Yeye
Titobi
Dancers, drummers, singers and musicians

*When play begins, spotlight comes on* IYA OLORISA.
*There is music, drums and praise chants of orisa ibeji in
the background.*


IYA OLORISA: Iba o!  Iba!
    Orisa Ibeji, iba!
    My goddess looms large … from
    The riverine swamp of Badagry to
    The earth of red clay… She looms.
    In paired shells of carved iroko wood
    Rich coral *ileke iyun* … adorns her neck …
    Her body shines, oiled in perfumed olive
    Covered in rich *aso-oke, etu* and *sanyan,*
    her tribal marks, deep set
    distinct and of royal lineage of Olodumare …
    Haa! See how she looms large!
    What a wondrous sight to behold
    Yeye Ibeji mi o!
    In your kind and gentle smile
    I see how you radiate
    the wealth of kindness which flows
    through … until it touches us all
    far … far into a distant land
    Heralding the birth of twinned visitors of grace.
    So, I greet you
    Ejire ara Isokun
    Edunjobi aromose.
    I say thank you for your
    Twins; playful, stubborn,
    Devious and full of trickery that make
    Elegbara, sometimes, a better playmate.

Kabiyesi! ... Iba!
Haa … Iya mi o! Orisa Ibeji mi o!
Oninu ire lo n bi edun lomo
Won ni ki edun san
Wo ile o ko o ni kaka
Ki oun san
Oun a san wo origi.  Haa, Yeye …
Today, your stern eyes frighten me.
Why do you look so angry?
Who dares the other side of my mother?
Who? Ibeko *ke*?
Those descendant riff-raff from Itesi ke?
Let them feel your anger then, Yeye.
Yes, the Ibeko people force your hand, and
whoever defies the goddess  faces her
damning wrath.
First, they stopped her worship
They even treated her gifts of joy
with disdain in their palace.
And threw me … Iya Olorisa … out to the
outskirts of the town like a poxed reject.
Me!
To this end, they shall know no peace.
Yeye, listen to your faithful, Iya Olorisa,
Listen to the voice of your shamed servant.
Becloud their lives with darkness,
Until you are fully re-enthroned.
And the Olori dances with *ere ibeji* to the
market square in tune with *dundun* drums.
Let their *akisa* remain shredded and torn.
Do not turn them; those miserable poor
wearers of  torn  smelly clothes, and  spent

Empty coffers of Ibeko into
Onigba aso. Never!  Yeye,
I say never!

*(Slowly, spotlight goes off.)*

*Lights reveal the inner chamber of the king. He is seated on a stool, and three other chiefs, OLUAWO, OTUN and JAGUNA, listen to him.*

ADEDIGBA: I awoke to the shrills of a thousand sounds ... the grunts of the spirits who keep watch over my royal head, muttering cries of entities of the endless world of our sacred ancestors. Alone, I lay bare like a dog, sacrificed at the altar of Ogun.

OLUAWO: Kabiyesi o.

ADEDIGBA: Yes, Oluawo. Only this time my hands were tied; not with a cheap twine but with the red royal coral bead, iyun. Alone, I was waiting for the axe of the Abore ... to have my head taken off.

OTUN: Ewo, Kabiyesi! A thousand cutlasses would not cut. Never! Not your royal neck, Kabiyesi! Ewo!

ADEDIGBA: Not as I lay there, Otun. My mouth gagged, my eyes swollen with blood and sweat. My tongue dry, and my heart racing to the valley of death ahead of my soul. I say I looked stretched like *ebo* Ogun.

OLUAWO: Where was Olori Mojisola, Kabiyesi? I left both of you in the chamber. She was to rub the ointment on her stomach.

ADEDIGBA: There. She was there before my eyes shut. Now, so heavy with child, her chatter emptied my patience as best as it could, leaving a tiredness on my brow. Ha! Oluawo, weakened, my spirits failed me.

OLUAWO: How, Kabiyesi?

ADEDIGBA: A stare!

OLUAWO: A stare?

ADEDIGBA: A stare, Oluawo. A chilly stare from Iku's pointed nib of death.

OLUAWO: By whom, Kabiyesi?

ALL: Ha!

ADEDIGBA: Death himself came down to our world tonight. To the depth of my soul, even though I was calm.

OLUAWO: And very much so, Kabiyesi. Death cannot touch you. You know all his names. He would not dare embrace you.

ADEDIGBA: But he came. Afraid of nothing, he came.

OLUAWI: Yes, Kabiyesi … just to see you … he only came to visit, I am sure. A nudge, a reminder of his supreme existence. Both of you parted ways the day you became king. He, to the left and you, to the right. That is why you do not set eyes on his victims. Ewo!

ADEDIGBA: But he came! Would I lie?

OLUAWO: Not for you I am sure. Anyway, did you offer him a little sacrifice when you awoke?

ADEDIGBA: No. By the time he left, I knew better.

OLUAWO: You knew what better, Kabiyesi?

ADEDIGBA: That I was the sacrifice.

OLUAWO: Ewo!

OTUN: Please do not mind Oluawo, Kabiyesi. Tell us about this dream which frightened you, the lion of our people, so much, you summoned us in the middle of the night. Tell us, Kabiyesi. Abese was frantic in delivering the message. In my house, he whispered it in a breathless voice. I had started to prepare myself for … the worst … but I thank the gods we met you well.

ALL: Otun!

OTUN: Er, may Ogun forbid … but he caused me to worry. Hmm. Anyway, now that we are here, it is only fair that we hear it delivered well. Talk, Kabiyesi.

ALL: Yes, Kabiyesi.

ADEDIGBA: Very well.

OLUAWO: Kabiyesi. I beg for your forgiveness.

ADEDIGBA: All of a sudden, a cold, chilly silence fell. I now really felt alone. My right hand searching for the waist of Olori … but alas, she was gone.

OTUN: Gone to where?

ADEDIGBA: Slowly, my eyelids opened fully to the new emptiness of the vacant royal chamber. I wore nothing but my small white cap, a white top cloth and a large white wrapper … like I am dressed now. Coldness seized my limbs, my throat dry, I wanted a drop of water badly ... just a drop to quench the ... thirst to restore my senses ...

OTUN: How about your usual water bowl, Kabiyesi?

*(Pointing to the bowl on the table. He goes to the table.)*

ADEDIGBA: Empty.

OTUN: But it is full to the brim.

ADEDIGBA: Emptiness filled the whole space in my dream. Searching for people ... anyone ... I left this room. Tired by the spirit of fear of the unknown. The emptiness filled everywhere ... Not a soul. From room to room I wandered ... not a single soul. As I stepped out of the living quarters, I heard shrill muffled laughter, as if they were made by caged-up masquerades of the gods. High-pitched nasal sounds by the nostrils from pipes of bones like awakened zombies deafened my ears ... The sound filled me up with fear...raw fear that would make even a king wet his wrapper.

OTUN: Kabiyesi, no!

ADEDIGBA: The sound came from the Oju Orori of the Obas. The sacred room of the kings before me. I moved closer.

OLUAWO: Haa! Ewo, Kabiyesi! You are forbidden to go there until it is time for you to rest forever. Ewo, Kabiyesi!

ADEDIGBA: The sound called me. Deserted, vultures had taken over the sky ... my white wrapper drenched in sweat, wrapped with dirty wool

15

from the web of cobwebs. I was trapped beyond myself. I had become one with the shrill sound which repeatedly was forming a pattern … a high flown rhythm of jeers and call of shame on its listener. Again, I moved closer, even as my spirit had started to ebb away. I moved closer …

OLUAWO: No, Kabiyesi!

ADEDIGBA: With a clenched left fist, I broke the door open … tore down the red long cloth and the *mariwo* sacred palm tree leaves drape … there. Behold, they were there … all of them.

OTUN: Who, Kabiyesi?

ADEDIGBA: The kings before me, past Obas. Their skulls clean, not a sight of flesh … eyes plucked out … just mere bones. Then a black crow flew past my face … for a second … I saw their faces. I recognized the ones I knew … sadly my father, Oba Adebimpe, and then me.

OLUAWO: You? But …

ADEDIGBA: Yes.

OLUAWO: How can? The living has nothing to do with the resting-place of the dead. You cannot be there without … being dead. Ewo!

ADEDIGBA: I know what I saw. I saw myself.

OLUAWO: Yes, Kabiyesi.

ADEDIGBA: My head was cut off by a blunt cutlass. The cut was forced. I was like a bloody ring of dripping blood round the neck of the head.

OLUAWO: Ewo ... Do not claim the death of a blunt cutlass, Kabiyesı.

ADEDIGBA: But I know what I saw. *(Pause.)* I turned with a painful stiffness on my neck; he kept saying that he was innocent of the reason why he was killed. And that I made him die in my place. And he swore to have me join him soon.

OLUAWO: Your head said all that, Kabiyesi?

ADEDIGBA: My own head. My sawn-off head.

OLUAWO: Ewo, Kabiyesi! What did you do?

ADEDIGBA: I ran out of the room. *(Pause.)*
To the palace well.

OTUN: The well? Which well?

ADEDIGBA: But when I got to the palace well, I met an old woman crying. Her eyes sunk in, red, flowing with tears. She carried a small calabash of water. I ran to her begging her for a drink from my own well. Slowly, she looked at me. "You again," she said. "You ungrateful animal," she said. "Instead of giving you a drop of this water, I would rather do this." With one swipe, she broke the calabash on the dry earth. My mouth was wide open, amazed at the depth of her anger. I have never met this woman in my life. As I turned in anger to ask her for the reason of her action, she jumped into the well, cursing as she fell. The gods forgive me. Who have I offended? What have I done wrong? Why would my own head announce my own death to me? Oluawo, tell Ajagunmale the oracle man of the heavens to save me ... I must not be allowed to become an imbecile to the land of my ancestors. Not I, Oba Adedigba ... not I. You have heard my song of fear. This is why I have brought you here this late ... sorry, this early in the morning.

OLUAWO: Haa, Kabiyesi!

ADEDIGBA: Jaguna.

JAGUNA: Kabiyesi o!

ADEDIGBA: You are the head of the kingmakers. By the oath of your office, was there any reason why I was not supposed to be crowned king?

JAGUNA: None, Kabiyesi. Your father, Oba Adebimpe, the king before you, had twenty-six daughters and one son. You were that son. The only heir-apparent. We crowned you as custom demanded.

ADEDIGBA: Was Ifa consulted?

JAGUNA: There was no need, Kabiyesi. There was just one of you. No confusion arose. Even the gods attested to it. You were the only male child ... the only candidate. You would have been made king even if your Odu was one vote. The kingmakers found picking and crowning you as king the easiest job so far. You came in the right way, Kabiyesi.

ADEDIGBA: And the gods?

JAGUNA: They were all consulted. Their sacrifices offered. They stood by us all through the time of the

*Ipebi*. The preparation period was also smooth. You chose a good name. Adedigba ... the crown multiplics its blessings twentyfold ... You chose honey to symbolize the sweetness of your reign. We danced and sang in happiness because every other thing in the calabashes you chose, were in twofolds; double joy, Kabiyesi. The gods had a hand in your choice and they assured us of a long, great and peaceful reign.

ADEDIGBA: If I came in properly, as you claim, and the gods assured me of a good and long harvest, why the attack of this swarm of locusts on my farm? Why?

*(Balogun enters with* IFADUNBE.*)*

BALOGUN: Kabiyesi, we went to the land of Oni as you said we should, but we were told that Ifagbayi, the great seer, had died three days ago. We were then advised to come with Ifadunbe, a formidable priest, also.

ADEDIGBA: Welcome. Very well, then. You say he is highly recommended?

BALOGUN: Yes, Kabiyesi.

ADEDIGBA: *(Chuckles.)* But his name, Ifadunbe.

IFADUNBE: Yes, Kabiyesi. Ifadunbe aiye mi. Ifa sweetens the pot of soup of my life.

ADEDIGBA: Good, as long as you know that the matter at hand is serious, not food. Balogun, have you told him everything?

BALOGUN: Everything, Kabiyesi. He has come prepared.

ADEDIGBA: Very well, then. Please speak to the gods. I am anxious to know.

IFADUNBE: *(Begins to consult the oracle.)* Haa … this is strange. Two heads as one, tied with the knot of life. Um. The harm has been done … we now must appease the one we offended.

ADEDIGBA: With what, Ifadunbe, with what? Speak, Ifadunbe. What sacrifices do we make? I must live to be an old man … speak.

IFADUNBE: You miss your loss. The royal carver is to carve your head. Exact shape, nose and all. And once you are two again, you shall be well and happy.

ADEDIGBA: This *baba* is mad. A carving of my head?

IFADUNBE: Yes, Kabiyesi.

OLUAWO: What else, Baba? A carving of Kabiyesi's head and nothing else?

IFADUNBE: Nothing, Kabiyesi. The gods ask for nothing. You have forgiven yourself. Ifa says no sacrifices will be needed, but we must take sweet things. Sugar cane, honey, *aadun*, and sweet beans, *akara* and palm oil to the shrine of Orisa Ibeji.

ADEDIGBA: What rubbish does this old fool speak of? Orisa Ibeji *ke*? The village is not at peace and you speak of Orisa Ibeji. My story is not about twins. I don't know of one. We forbid them in this palace. Keep your mind focused on what Balogun told you, old man. Who forgave who? Speak, old man!

IFADUNBE: You, Kabiyesi. You must forgive yourself. If

you remain still, and do nothing, you will not live. Carry the calabash of sweet things yourself, and say before the Orisa Ibeji that you forgive yourself, and you shall live.

ADEDIGBA: That I forgive myself?

IFADUNBE: Yes. Kabiyesi. Ifa says, what do we worship in Ile-Ife? Mouth ... enu, enu lan bo ni Ife, enu. I take the orogbo nuts, I take the abata nuts. I say what do they worship in Ile- Ife? Mouth ... enu, enu lan bo ni Ile-Ife. Enu! A party to celebrate your life will then hold.

ADEDIGBA: *(Angry, rises.)* Abese! Abese!

ABESE: *(Runs in.)* Yes, my lord.

ADEDIGBA: Take this stupid old hungry fool out of my sight. Hurry! Oluawo, find a better Ifa priest please.

*(Sharp lights off as ABESE carries out IFADUNBE.)*

*In the throne room. When lights come on, OBA ADEDIGBA is asleep. Three elderly women appear. They look at the sleeping body of OBA ADEDIGBA with amazement. They confirm that he is the person. IKATE steps forward.*

IKATE: Impostor, awake! The Mothers want to talk with you.

YINYIN: Oba Adedigba, we say awake!

ADEDIGBA: *(Wakes.)* Who dares to wake me up?

BANTE: We dare. An impostor does not become king. A dead king does not rule.

ADEDIGBA: A dead king? Impostor! Me?

IKATE: Yes, you.

YINYIN: The dead has nothing to do with the living. Nothing!

ADEDIGBA: I still do not understand.

IKATE: We do, because we three were all there. We saw you shared like a sacrifice to reawaken the spirit of life. We saw you gasp for life, and in despair, die. We saw your carcass, though living, walk down the battlefield, dazed, drunk and fallen. We saw your Balogun, further smitten by the madness of victory, with a blunt sword, remove your head, and dance home to his fellow foes. We saw it all.

ADEDIGBA: Me?

YINYIN: I say we saw you. With our six eyes, we all saw you.

22

IKATE: So what are you doing, spread like the now late headless king in the royal chamber, on the royal bed? Answer, impostor!

ADEDIGBA: Impostor ... haa, now it appears clearer to me. I remember the night you speak of as if it was yesterday. It was Orija, the village before Atiba. We had fought all day, and my men were getting tired of the war. I too had become exhausted. The rains did not help either. It beat my charms and war dress and crown. One day, I had them laid out to dry. But the soldiers of Atiba came and stole them. In the face of such a disaster, and with me unprotected, I was smuggled out of the battlefield. But my dress and crown were taken to Balogun Atiba, whom I heard had to celebrate his victory. He wore them, got drunk, sang and danced all night, until he slept with them still on him. When you came to take me, you must have thought you took me. Remember it was a hazy, murky and dark night, Mothers.

YINYIN: Hazy enough to deceive us? Come on, Oba Adedigba, we may be women, but we are not fools. I say we know what we saw. You.

BANTE: And we see clearest in the haziest of nights.

IKATE: We know whose soul we took. We know what shell we left behind ... the living carcass of a king. Or ... haaa, Mothers, come closer, I smell deceit here. *(The women gather. She whispers. They all gasp. She turns sharply to ADEDIGBA.)* Impostor, are there two of you?

23

ADEDIGBA: Two of me? I don't understand.

IKATE: Don't pretend not to be a twin. We abhor twins. We loathe them. Don't try to fool us because the secret you intend to hide from us may choke you first. I say, do you have a twin brother?

ADEDIGBA: Me? The gods forbid. You all know what would have happened to me even at birth. What silly thoughts possess you, Mothers?

BANTE: Then why did ... Why did Orisa Ibeji try to fool us with two effigies that look like one? Why give up one and protect the other ... you from us? Or did she?

ADEDIGBA: My dear mothers Osoromoniga! Owners of the night ... how am I to know? How was I to know the ways of the goddess?

IKATE: Impostor!

BANTE: Sisters. Could Esu Odara have sold us out? Why would Esu Odara do this to us, after we all swore to destroy Oba Adedigba for his deceit?

AEDIGBA: Swore! But, why? What have I done to anger the gods for them to want to share me as if I were a piece of cloth?

BANTE: You really don't know?

AEDIGBA: I swear by my forefathers, I do not know ... What came over you? I thought I was your favourite son. You promised to keep me and watch over me before my coronation. Now you call me names. Why? I am still a man of honour ... I swear!

BANTE: *(Lets out a wild laugh.)* Honour, my foot! My dog has more honour than a king who connives with an Orisa to fool Death. *(Chuckles.)* Honour?

ADEDIGBA: So, Mothers, what will happen to me now?

IKATE: Death again … but this time it shall be slower, until your new god cries for you, and bleeds blood.

ADEDIGBA: Mothers, please!

BANTE: Now you beg again. The same voice you used when we first had you. You must see us as fools, or blind imbeciles fooled by treacherous gods and kings who lie … We shall get you.

YINYIN: Mothers, Mothers … still your spirits. Not here. Not now. We can still find him by the market square eating his spoils. Hurry before he leaves.

IKATE: Impostor, we shall return soon. We must know how it happened. You, a king, who wronged us and was found guilty and condemned to death, would connive with Death and still live. The finger of a god must be in this, and we shall find whose. We shall return, impostor. If you are wrong and we find that Olodumare, the only god we fear, does not have a hand in this deceit, we shall return with a rage fit only to roast you alive. And this time, you shall not be able to escape the rage of fury that will encircle your soul. Away, Mothers, hurry!

ADEDIGBA: Abese!

ABESE: *(Hurries in.)* My lord!

ADEDIGBA: Abese, call me Oluawo at the break of dawn. Hurry!

*(Sharp darkness.)*

*In the throne room.* OLUAWO *and* ADEDIGBA *are seated.*

ADEDIGBA: They appeared, my mothers Osoromoniga ... all with twisted faces ... angry, demanding to know who I was.

OLUAWO: What rubbish talk! Who you are? Does an elephant announce itself? Does the moon roar before lighting up its presence? You should have told them, Kabiyesi, that you are Oba Adedigba, son of Oba Adebimpe ... son of Oba Adebambo, son of ... Oba Lempe.

ADEDIGBA: You think they don't know all that?

OLUAWO: Then why did they ask? I hope you answered them word for word, Kabiyesi?

ADEDIGBA: I could not find my voice that easily. Not in the presence of those women. They called me an impostor. Repeatedly, they accused me of pretending to be Oba Adedigba. Me! King of Ibeko! Me!

OLUAWO: You should have called me, Kabiyesi. I would have explained it better to them.

ADEDIGBA: *(Chuckles.)* Explain? To whom? I say they were not sane. Angered, they said they were fooled. As they spoke, it became clear that they had killed the spirit of Balogun Atiba in error, instead of killing Adedigba. They swore to get to the root of the matter. They even accused Esu Odara of deceiving them. I could taste their scorn ... it reeled of bile.

OLUAWO: Esu Odara *ke?*

ADEDIGBA: Yes. They promised to return if they found out that I was indeed an impostor. Oluawo, what do I do? All the gods are against me!

OLUAWO: (*Pause.*) Impostor? Esu Odara? How could he change sides so quickly? He promised to stand by us to the end. He asked for a fat he-goat, and you ordered that we should give him a cow. Even the Mothers got one, too. So, what happened? Why the mix-up? Take heart, Kabiyesi. It is failure to look far that makes a person claim that a hunchback squirrel does not exist. I think we should start from the beginning.

ADEDIGBA: What do we do, Oluawo?

OLUAWO: Let us go to the shrine of Esu Odara.

ADEDIGBA: It is not possible. Me, at the shrine of Esu Odara? After the disgrace I gave Saura, his Chief Priest? Oluawo, I shall be shamed out of the shrine house. I cannot go.

OLUAWO: Disgrace?

ADEDIGBA: Several times he has been to the palace to see me, and I refused to see him. Saura does not know when to come visiting. I even cancelled the festival for this year. Oluawo, I say I cannot go.

OLUAWO: You can go, Kabiyesi. You must go! We need to know. We must save your neck from the noose of death.

ADEDIGBA: I cannot. The jeers of the people will follow me all the way to the shrine. Saura will dance and sing on my return to beg. He could even make me, Oba Adedigba, go on my knees to beg him. And I heard him swear, the last time he came here never to step foot here again. That old man is stubborn. How can we achieve this impossible act, Oluawo? How?

OLUAWO: I think I know how we can go without anybody finding out. *(Chuckles.)* Even the great Esu Odara will be fooled this once.

ADEDIGBA: You say we shall escape the jeers of the people?

OLUAWO: Like chameleons, Kabiyesi, we shall dance in colours and shades that soothe the mood of blindness. Like chameleons, we shall change and be dainty enough, moving gently to the beat of deceit. The people can only know you if they identify us. Kabiyesi … *(Moves closer to* ADEDIGBA *and whispers into his ear.)* This is what we shall do …

ADEDIGBA: Umm … good idea. Tonight then, when darkness becomes a convenient cloak, we shall do it. *(Just then,* IYALODE *runs in.)*

IYALODE: Kabiyesi o!

ADEDIGBA: Iyalode … you pant.

IYALODE: My ears are full, Kabiyesi.. The whole village is not at peace. The women are crying.

ADEDIGBA: *(Turns to* OLUAWO.*)* Crying? Oluawo, have you heard their cries?

OLUAWO: Kabiyesi, let Iyalode say it with her own mouth.

ADEDIGBA: Iyalode, speak.

IYALODE: Women die in childbirth, Kabiyesi. Children in various twisted shapes are born. Instead of joy and happiness, houses cry, sorrow reigns supreme, Kabiyesi.

ADEDIGBA: Did you ask Ifa why all these ills are befalling the women in the village?

IYALODE: I did, Kabiyesi.

OLUAWO: What did Ifa say?

IYALODE: The gods are angry, Kabiyesi. Sacrifice must be carried to the centre of the village in the middle of the night. Before it leaves the palace, Kabiyesi must pray for protection for the women of the village. He must call his mother's name, Olori Titubi, and beg her for forgiveness.

ADEDIGBA: Is that all?

IYALODE: Yes, Kabiyesi.

ADEDIGBA: Then hurry to Abore. Tell him what to do. I shall wait for them tonight. Hurry!

IYALODE: I go, Kabiyesi.

OLUAWO: Tell him that I know about it. Hurry, woman!

ADEDIGBA: Oluawo, I fear my end may be coming to an end indeed.

OLUAWO: Ewo, Kabiyesi! I think we are beginning to uncover the clove of the *Ajopa* kolanut. The sweetness of your reign will follow soon, Kabiyesi.

ADEDIGBA: Um.

OLORI: *(OLORI MOJISOLA comes in, tired. She kneels.)* Kabiyesi o!

ADEDIGBA: Haa, Olori you came on time. Did you not meet your mother at home?

OLORI: No. Despite all the messages I sent, they said she left home at the break of dawn for the farm. She refused to return home even after I sent for her. So I left what I took for her and returned to the palace.

*(She sits, exhausted, next to the king.)*

ADEDIGBA: You are really tired.

OLORI: Very tired, Kabiyesi. A madwoman I have never met, who now stays by my mother's house chased us up and down the road, begging me to take her twin *ere ibeji* and give birth to them.

ADEDIGBA: She chased you? How about the Abese? Where were they? They were to protect you from harm.

OLORI: They did. But the madness of the woman was full-blown. She had the carved babies wrapped in her torn cloth. She pretended to be feeding them when we passed her to see my mother, but on our way back, she started to jump up and down, screaming at me. That these were my real babies … a blessed gift from her. And I should return to pick them up. Then she started to cry as we ignored her and started to walk very fast. It was then that the chase began …

ADEDGBA: The chase?

OLORI: Yes. But I could not run, so she caught up with me, and forced me to collect the carvings from her.

OLUAWO: No, Olori … Ewo!

OLORI: I was too weak to struggle with her.

AEDIGBA: I hope you gave it to the Abese to cut it into tiny bits and throw it into the big bush by the stream?

OLORI: I did not have the heart. I wrapped the carvings up like real children. She liked it as I fed them, which made her giggle. Then she made us sing,

"Be epo nbe, ewa n be o. Be epo nbe ewa nbe o. Aya mi o ja, o eh, ayami o ja latibi beji, be epo n be, ewan be o."

OLUAWO: No. With the song you accept them, Olori! No!

OLORI: (*Ignores him, just continues talking.*) I rocked them, until we both pretended they had slept off. At that time, Abese came with some foodstuff for her. We gave her. We even gave her some money. As we left, she cried after us. "Wait", she screamed … "Wait, daughter … wait for your Kehinde and your son, Taiye. Wait, they always go in pairs." Frustrated, she ran after us again. We hurried home. I am thirsty. I could drink a river!

(*Rises.*)

ADEDIGBA:   May the gods forbid. Who will take twin children from a madwoman? Twins in this palace? May the gods forbid! Ogun would have their heads at his shrine before you can sing your lullaby. Hurry in, go and wash off her mad touch on your royal presence. Quick, Olori. *(OLORI goes in.)* Oluawo, with madwomen distributing twins, pregnant women giving birth before their time, some with twisted  abnormal children, go to Abore, let him lead the cleansing *etutu* tonight to the gods of the land. There is a new wave of madness concerning children. An evil spirit which does not even respect the prescience of the Queen. Hurry! And, Oluawo, concerning our  planned visit to Suara tonight, where did we stop?

OLUAWO: Yes, Kabiyesi … I was going to suggest that we go with … *(As he whispers into the ear of ADEDIGBA, slowly, lights fade.)*

*Dark stage.* ABORE *leads three priests all in white priestly dresses with osugbo on their shoulders in. He holds a staff which he hits on the ground in rhythm with their walk. A young man in red wrapper carries a calabash of etutu.*

ABORE: Epa!

ALL: Epa mole!

ABORE: Epa!

ALL: Epa mole!

ABORE: A ki wo.
Eni ba wo!

ALL: A ku gbi!

ABORE: Leave it here. Gods of our land, the people of Ibeko sent us. They want you to receive this gift from us, and let us be in peace. Forgive us if we have offended you all. Our fathers, Aromire, Odunlade, Osinlokun, share in this. Take away the afflictions in the land. Let peace be restored to our lives. *(They turn to leave.)* Epa!

ALL: Epa mole!

ABORE: A kiwo!

ALL: Eni bawo, aku gbi!

MADWOMAN: *(As they exit, MADWOMAN comes in, opens the calabash, and lets out a wild laugh.)* The fools. They concentrate and try to cure mere ringworm instead of chronic leprosy. Stupid fools!

*(In anger, she turns the calabash upside down, still laughing wildly, she runs off the  stage. Light fades.)*

*Esu's shrine.* OBA ADEDIGBA, *dressed like a woman, stands, his back turned to the shrine. Enter* SAURA *with an oil lamp.*

SAURA: Woman, what needs drive you this time of the night, that you defy the fear of wakening my master? Have you no husband?

ADEDIGBA: I have, old one and children too. Those who sucked my breasts and when they became weaned felt an urge to discard their poor mother, and find another wife for their father.

SAURA: Egrets all.

ADEDIGBA: I am happy you see them for what and who they are.

SAURA: Have you told your husband … their father … about the animals he calls children?

ADEDIGBA: The children have outgrown fear.

SAURA: Hmmm … a domestic family matter, then. My master abhors women problems … they get too messy. We have other pressing matters at hand. Go, woman … go to the home of Iyalode where women's matters are celebrated.

ADEDIGBA: Iyalode ke? I thought Esu Odara was a good god for everyone. During his festival at the Oke Awo each year, the women dance more than the men, bringing more gifts and supplications. Most of all, they prepare his dish of *Ekuru* and palm oil. We. It is us who dance with Kabiyesi to the Orita Esu with his sacrifice to tamper less with our lives. Esu lalu laroye larogo. Akiriboto okunrin. Alekuru lega, alegakuru, alaya gbogbo ilu, laroye, la rogo.

SAURA: Stop, woman, stop! Oke Awo ke? Enough, woman. You chant like the woman who bares the igba Esu to the shrines. Your tongue touched by palm oil, glides ... you know too much. How come you know the content of the king's prayers at the shrine of Esu, how? Only three of us know this chant; the *Arugba*, who is deaf and dumb, the King and myself. Who are you, woman?

ADEDIGBA: A woman ... a mother ...

SAURA: No. I seem to know you well. Your voice beats a gong of remembrance. *(Walks close to him as if looking for something to give him away. Suddenly, he lets out a loud laugh.)* When did we start to crown women kings? Kabiyesi Adedigba, I welcome you to the home of Esu Odara. *(Chuckles.)* You amaze me, Kabiyesi. A king in a woman's dress! My master Lalu will laugh until he feels giddy; his beady eyes all red, and full of tears, will go all soggy at the sight of this clownish mannequin before me! *(Laughs again.)*

ADEDIGBA: I sent for you. And you refused to come.

SAURA: Can you remember how many times I came to see you in your magnificent palace?

ADEDIGBA: Ten times or more.

SAURA: Can you remember how many times out of the ten times or more we met to discuss or share palm-wine and kolanut like we used to, when you so desperately wanted to be king? Do you?

ADEDIGBA: I was busy with the affairs of governance.

SAURA: Oba Adedigba, what do you want from my master?

ADEDIGBA: Life.

SAURA: That you already have. I thought you were *ekeji orisha* ... second only to the supreme god, Olodumare.

ADEDIGBA: So I thought until I saw my headless body in a dream, announcing my death to me.

SAURA: Haa ... so you ran here when you discovered that your palace chant crier lies each time he says that you are second to the gods. It is a mere attempt to raise your ego, or when he says that as king you are death itself ... that you have conquered death? Iku ke? Then why do you climb the royal roof to take a final rest? Why? Ewo! No one conquers death. That is why the friendship of my master, Esu, and Death, Iku, remains forged, cast forever. What do you want, Kabiyesi?

ADEDIGBA: I want to live! I want the axe of death to dangle past my head. I want Esu to turn his eyes to the palace of my neighbour kings and let my palace be. I do not want to die.

SAURA: Again?

ADEDIGBA: Again? I do not understand.

SAURA: The Mothers of the night came to see my master.

Angry, they said you fooled them, and asked for your head. My master, pained by the similar trick of a sick chicken instead of a fat cow each, which you promised, assented to their requests.

ADEDIGBA: And so?

SAURA: You died, or so we heard the first time.

ADEDIGBA: I still do not understand.

SAURA: Why did you behead the Balogun of Atiba?

ADEDIGBA: In error. I did give the order in error. I was told that his men had stolen my war dress and crown. In anger and on impulse, I asked my Balogun for his head. And when he was captured at the battlefield the next day drunk and dazed, very unlike the legendary warrior we had heard about, in triumph, they did not bother to speak with me on the matter again. They simply beheaded him. I never saw it. But a strange thing happened just before my dream.

SARA: What?

ADEDIGBA: All the three war generals who supervised the beheading of the Balogun of Atiba were found strangled in their sleep. All three of them. In one night choked to death with akara in their mouths.

SAURA: How strange, indeed. You say that you never met Balogun of Atiba in his lifetime?

ADEDIGBA: No.

SAURA: Until he appeared in your dream?

ADEDIGBA: No. That was my head.

SAURA: I know. So you unwittingly helped the mothers of the night to complete the task. And invariably died the first time.

ADEDIGBA: You speak to me as a priest, I do not understand. How many times does a man die, old friend?

SAURA: Then you do not know.

ADEDIGBA: Know what? Speak plainly, friend.

SAURA: No. Not me. It is in the mouth of the elder that kolanut tastes better. You will ask your grandmother, Akuda, for the secret of the whistling palms. I cannot say, Kabiyesi!

ADEDIGBA: Yeye Akuda is dead! What do I ask her? What does she know, Saura?

SAURA: Kabiyesi, I have told you what to do. Please listen, Kabiyesi. Ask the question about your life, get the knowledge you went for, and leave her to the darkness of the crypt. Nothing more.

ADEDIGBA: Nothing more, I swear!

SAURA: Oluawo, the matter is in your hands.

OLUAWO: We hear you, Saura. May the gods guide us.

SAURA: Now go, while the darkness can still hide the disguise of the king. Hurry …

*(As they leave,* IKATE *appears from the shadow.)*

IKATE: I heard it all,

SAURA: What world is this turning into? The Mother of the night turning into an eavesdropper who listens to the stories of a heartbroken king? Um!

IKATE: I came to see your master. We want to know what happened. The Mothers are angry.

SAURA: *(Chuckles.)* I feel your anger from your voice. You even call my master names. Why?

IKATE: We agreed to have his soul after the rains, did we not?

SAURA: You did. But you failed my master.

IKATE: We did? *(Chuckles.)* After all the promises of a sacrifice of a cow each to us and your master Esu Odara, we found a sick chicken tied to the tree when we got there. Obviously, you got what you wanted ... a fat cow. That is why he can come to your shrine in confidence. Your master was not true with us.

SAURA: We, too. We got a sick chicken. For days, my master sneezed. Angered, on your behalf, he ran into the village creating a living hell amongst innocent people. For your sake, he killed a thousand chickens, and another thousand goats. Just for your sake.

IKATE: *Shio!* No one asked him to cry on our behalf. We can carry our load, no matter how heavy.

SAURA: I had to beg Orunmila to calm him down.

IKATE: Then why help him? Why send him to his grandmother's spirit? What do you want him to find out? Why clear the pathway for him?

SAURA: Did we help him? No. Instead, he shall find the woven noose that will end his life this time. My master is disappointed with the Mothers. You have failed my master to kill a common man.

MADWOMAN: *(Appears from the darkness.)* A common man, did you say?

IKATE: Who are you? How dare you? Saura, I thought you said this place was safe to talk.

MADWOMAN: No place is safe for you any more, Ikate. For the one you took, you committed a taboo. Ewo kabiti, kabiti!

IKATE: How dare you? She calls me by name? Is this a trick by Esu, Saura? How come she can see me? Where did a common madwoman get all these powers from? Why?

MADWOMAN: You and your kind offended my goddess. You took her sacred son.

IKATE: Your goddess? Who is she?

MADWOMAN: You took one of her own, and now she will clip your wings. Roast you all like forbidden birds, and throw you into the darkest part of hell.

SAURA: Who are you?

MADWOMAN: Keep quiet, old man. Tell your master, we shall talk after my return. When the rains stop. Soon, Saura, soon. *(Disappears into the darkness.)* When the people of Ibeko are brought to their knees. Soon, Saura!

SAURA: When a madwoman begins to speak as if she is normal, then the whole village is sick. Hurry home, Mother, I need to summon my master. Hurry!

*(Lights slowly fade.)*

*The ghost of a frail old woman, AKUDA, dressed in aso oke, appears. She is bent and almost speaks all her words in a whisper.*

AKUDA: *(Her back turned to both men.)* Who wakes me from the slumber of death?

OLUAWO: Kabiyesi Adedigba ... the King of ...

AKUDA: I don't know him. Is he here?

OLUAWO: Yes.

AKUDA: Where is he? My eyes fail me. Or does he send baskets of troubled souls through the mouth of an *Ilari*?

OLUAWO: Ilari ke? No, Yeye Akuda. I am Oluawo, head of the Awo cult. Those close to earth, but closer to the spirits of the world. He sent me to awaken you.

AKUDA: This king of yours, has he no mouth of his own?

OLUAWO: He has, Yeye. *(Turns to ADEDIGBA. Pushes him forward.)* Here, Mama, he stands behind you. *(She begins to turn slowly until she faces ADEDIGBA. ADEDIGBA jerks out of fear. In a whisper.)* Kabiyesi, remain still ... very still.

AKUDA: *(Slowly, AKUDA feels ADEDIGBA'S face with her two hands. Like a blind person, she feels his nose, mouth, every shape of his face.)* He appears familiar to me. A distant face. But his blood smells like mine. He reminds me of when I had some blood running down my veins, and life was mine to breathe. Oh, I must have slept for too long. My eyelids flicker on their own. Mine slowly, dissolving, I forget faces now. And my eyes blur. You say he is the king who summoned me? Does he know me?

OLUAWO: Yes, Queen Mother. Akuda Subuladc Eso, old woman who knows the names of death. Akinkaju obirin who lives in the deep red sea. Ajile opo. The woman from the house where the cheapest gifts are rich coral beads. Faderera Akuda Odindin … a woman like a man. Who gave her blood for life. Ogugu Obanga, who gave her life for a tiger, Balogun Ogunkoroju of Atiba to pounce and devour the world. A woman …

AKUDA: Sssh! You know me. What does the Kabiyesi want from me?

OLUAWO: The Kabiyesi wants …

AKUDA: He has a voice of his own, doesn't he? Let him speak!

OLUAWO: Very well, speak, Kabiyesi.

AKUDA: Be brief though. I embark on a long trip soon, and I need all my strength for it. Be brief, King.

ADEDIGBA: Life.

AKUDA: Um?

ADEDIGBA: I want to live, Yeye Akuda.

AKUDA: *(Lets out a wild loud laugh.)* You come to the wrong person, child. How can you ask for that? I am but a lifeless living carcass of a once-lived spirit. In short, I am dead … a ghost … lifeless. How then can I give what I do not have, Son? How?

ADEDIGBA: Er … Yeye. I was sent to you. He said only you could give it to me.

AKUDA: Give what to you, son? Please lift your tongue and speak clearly. I do not have all day. Go straight to the issue, child.

ADEDIGBA: Life.

AKUDA: Nonsense! Utter nonsense! Who said such rubbish and sent you, a king?

ADEDIGBA: Saura … the servant of …

AKUDA: I know who he serves. (Pause.) What a world this is turning out to be. What a world where even a god cannot keep his word for long anymore. We had a pact. Esu and I. Not a word. We swore! I gave Esu his sacrifice, and we were to have sealed lips for life. (Chuckles.) For life. (Chuckles again.) I must have been a fool to trust him. But a gullible woman and the trickster king are a perfect match for deceit. I should have known that when a beautiful goddess like Orisa Ibeji confronted him, he would change his loyal garb and leave me broken. The very reason why l loathe this weakened frame!

ADEDIGBA: Orisa Ibeji, Yeye?

AKUDA: Yes, Orisa Ibeji. My daughter Titubi had made offerings at her shrine for the nine months she was pregnant. Orisa Ibeji was taken in by her dedication.

46

Forgetting that Titubi was an Olori of the Palace. The goddess of twins blessed her womb with two sons. I was unaware of what had taken place, but Orisa Ibeji was angered by my machinations to avert the sad edges of the law of the land. She swore to avenge my separation of her double gifts by making me drown in the ripples of my motherly kindness. I hear she left a curse in your palace.

ADEDIGBA: A curse, Yeye?

AKUDA: Is your wife pregnant?

ADEDIGBA: Yes, after all these years of waiting. The people had started to jeer. Even now, her big stomach is in its thirteenth month.

AKUDA: The strange woman again.

ADEDIGBA: Umm? What did you say, Yeye?

AKUDA: Nothing ... Just a fear. Hurry to her after this meeting, Kabiyesi. With me already punished with death and you dragged to a clownish level in the village, Orisa Ibeji may take pity on you and forgive you soon.

OLUAWO: I pray so, Yeye.

AKUDA: Believe me. I did what I did to save your lives. I swear! But before everything happened, I extracted a renewal of the oath from Ilari Akanji.

*(Dim lights on* ILARI *and* AKUDA.*)*

AKUDA: *(Pulls out a dagger.)* Ilari Akanji alasiri Oba. Remember that you swore to keep the secrets of the Oba and now me. Do not deceive me. Swear again to me and the gods.

ILARI: Ife ti Esu Odara ni fun Orunmila
Lo fi di olori didan.
Eti Oba ni le
Eti Oba loko
Ilari lonje be.
May my tongue not break this oath,
May my heart remain bound.
I stand by my oath to the Oba,
And transfer my oath to you. To the death.

*(He collects the dagger from her and kisses it. Lights on them slowly fade. Dim lights reveal pregnant TITUBI writhing in chidbirth pains on a bed made of bamboo. AKUDA tries to help the birth, cares for the pregnant woman. Two young maidens help her.)*

AKUDA: Push, daughter! Clasp your teeth like the true Queen that you are, and muffle the screams! Push, girl, let the pain seep through the tendons of your veins so that the joy of motherhood will reign. I say, push, Omolewa, Tumininu opo! Kabiyesi awaits our news. I say, out with the gift of Olodumare, woman, and let the cries of our long-awaited heir fill the palace space. Push, child!

IYUN: Yeye, I worry. Her eyes, even her breathing, is too fast. This is not a good sign. By now, she should have had the child. She grows weak, Yeye.

TADE: We should have called Iya Agbomola. By now, the baby would have arrived with less pains.

AKUDA: Umm. What can she do that we cannot do? I thought they said you were her slave before you came here?

TADE: Yes, Yeye. But she did not teach me this.

AKUDA: Teach you what?

TADE: How to refuse to accept what I feel.

AKUDA: I do not understand, Tade.

TADE: I cannot feel one child. The whole stomach is filled up with limbs. Stretched like a drum. Full of hands, legs and heads. This is all so confusing. I fear the Queen has a set of ...

AKUDA: *Sshii!* Shut your rotten mouth!

TADE: But I know what I feel, Yeye.

IYUN: Ewo! It cannot be. It is forbidden in the palace to feel more than one head in the stomach of an Olori. They will kill them both, remember?

AKUDA: Wait, let me see. *(She kneels by the queen's stomach and begins to feel.)* After I have first killed you both. Stop chattering and face the birth of my grandson. I feel only one. Ifagbayi had said the birth will be difficult. Damn her head, girl! What did you expect? An easy birth? This is a Prince, remember? Iyun, call me the Ilari waiting outside the door. *(Exit IYUN.)*

Now, tell me how your old midwife teacher used to

49

deliver little naughty babies who lie across their mother's wombs this way.

TADE: She used to tempt the child with a chant, then she would break into a song, and the child would come out dancing, turning first to the position the gods intended it to, guided, cajoled, pleaded with, and then out it would come. With its head it would glide out, without a tear, but a pampered chuckle … but these ones, Yeye … I fear, so I dare not think.

AKUDA: Then don't. Feel, guide, even cajole, but don't think, girl. Separate this baby from my child. I begin to worry. You remember what the old seer Ifagbayi said. The longer the water stays in the mother's calabash, the greater the possibility of the calabash breaking and pouring out its content.

TADE: I worry, Mother … *(Damping the head of the OLORI.)* Tell me, Yeye, why are twins not born in the palace in this village? In my village, twins are seen as double blessings from Olodumare. For two weeks, we dance and sing to welcome them.

AKUDA: Here, they kill them. But in my mother's village, Atiba, we worship them.

TADE: Kill them? But why?

AKUDA: Some stupid story about a set of twins who fought for the crown, until they killed half of the village. So the elders of the land decreed that all the twins born in the palace must be beheaded. What a foolish way to resolve a problem!

TADE: The gods will have their way today. Olori has a

set of twins in her. I am sure you know, Yeye.

AKUDA: Yes.

TADE: Was that why you did not invite Yeye Osun to come and help with the delivery?

AKUDA: Yes. But I was told that only you can deliver them. I shall pay you well, Tade. And I shall also set you free. Ilari shall take you to the outskirts of your village, Itakumosa, and set you free forever.

TADE: *(Kneels.)* Haa, Yeye. I will do it. I am sure I can do it.

AKUDA: Do it, Tade, and let us give my child the freedom she deserves from these boys who worry her soul. Free her, Tade, and I shall reward you.

TADE: Yes, Yeye. I need Iyun.

AKUDA: Leave her alone. She might be late. Tell me what to do.

TADE: Then come, Yeye, hold her two legs. Firmly. Set them apart. Do not loosen your grip, even if she weeps blood. Hold her tight, Yeye. Push, Olori!

*(Lights return to the room – OLUAWO's room.)*

AKUDA: I held tight, urging my daughter the Olori to push. I was ready for her death. All I wanted were my grandchildren.

ADEDIGBA: Grandchildren. Why?

OLUAWO: Hush, Kabiyesi. Hush … let her talk.

AKUDA: Tade started to sing, and with her two dainty

hands she started to touch and guide the children in Olori's womb tenderly. The movement started slowly. First, an outpour of blood and green grime, then a little head. I pulled him out gently, the second pushing his buttocks with his weak legs. At this point, Olori fainted, her breath in slow beats. Her life, slowly ebbing. Quickly before the children could cry, I took each one and blocked their little mouths with each breath. They sucked them, hungry and tired from the trip from heaven. My daughter died as they sucked. Quickly, I wrapped the birth sack into a calabash, wiped the place clean, called Ilari to take Tade out and bury the two of them.

ADEDIGBA: The two of them?

AKUDA: Iyun and Tade. To keep the secret sealed, they both had to die. I promised them freedom. Death was the ultimate freedom for a slave. I had them killed.

ADEDIGBA: But, Yeye …

OLUAWO: Hush, Kabiyesi.

AKUDA: My heart reached out to both innocent souls. But I left one. The one who looked more like their father. The second, I took. With my Ilari, we left for my mother's village, Atiba.

ADEDIGBA: Hmm.

AKUDA: So now that you have heard the truth, why do you disturb my slumber? Hurry. I return soon.

ADEDIGBA: Return, Yeye?

AKUDA: To the world of the living. I have asked to be deaf and dumb this time. And I want to be a man.

ADEDIGBA: A man? But as woman, you rose to become a myth. Abijawara, they call you. Obirin bi okurin. Jagajuga Akuda Eje, tiin npa okurin lekun.

AKUDA: *(Chuckles.)* Still, if only they knew the pains I took to earn that chant. If only they knew how many taboos I broke to become a man. No, not again. I have asked Olodumare for a destiny of silence on my second coming. But …

ADEDIGBA: But? Yeye, speak.

AKUDA: I want you to help me with a favour.

ADEDIGBA: What favour, Yeye?

AKUDA: Bury my last body, so that it can rest, and then I can get a new one before I am allowed to return to earth.

OLUAWO: Where can we find your body? The whole of Atiba searched for you. And when our soldiers plundered Atiba, we were told that the only way we could save the life of Kabiyesi for killing their Balogun, we needed to find your body, deify you and make sacrifices, to your spirit so that you could forgive us, and erase the pact you made with Esu. We could not find it. Where is it, Yeye?

ADEDIGBA: Yes … this is all we came for. Where can we find you, Yeye?

AKUDA: The bottom of the well in your palace. My son drained my blood, and was asked to drop me there, urged on by a strange woman. She had told him to do that to acquire more power.

OLUAWO: A strange woman?

ADEDIGBA: He killed you just to acquire more power?

AKUDA: Yes. Power was his weakness. This strange woman came from nowhere. Immediately my son set his eyes on her, she took my place. He did anything she wanted. She hated me on sight too. I could feel it.

ADEDIGBA: Yeye, who am I? Taiwo or Kehinde? And what happened to the Ilari?

AKUDA: I killed him. I needed a lamb for sacrifice for the protection of both of you. I told him, and he gave himself up as it was his duty and oath to your father. *(Clears her throat.)* As for you, come closer again. *(ADEDIGBA moves closer to her. She begins to feel his face.)* Ejire ara Isokun, Oyilaki Oba omo, Ajifiluki. Bu mi ki mba o r'ele,
Yin mi, ki npada sehin, Ejire afinju omo.
Okan ni mba bi, eji wole
to mi, Kehinde elemele Akogunomo niise
Ajifiluki. You are Kehinde. The second one.
Haa … by the gods you should not have been King. You were born to be second only to your brother, Tayelolu. Ijo l'owo. Ejire ijo l'orole.
No wonder!

ADEDIGBA: What, Yeye?

AKUDA: He tried too hard to prove himself. And even when I thought he had enough power to take on

54

the world, he used me as sacrifice.

ADEDIGBA: Sacrifice, Yeye?

AKUDA: A pinch, he said. Just enough to take a little of my blood. How was I to know that he needed all my blood? I watched him drain all my blood, every drop of it. And as I died, I cursed him to a painful forced death. Even as the strange woman stood by him, jeering. *(Pause.)* Pray, how did my son die?

ADEDIGBA: Just the way you cursed him, Yeye. Advised, by a whisper of anger, my Balogun who now swears he never did, had someone take on his person, and urged me to go to war. I waged war against the people of Atiba against the wish of my common sense, even after the Ifa priest had warned me against it.

AKUDA: Another person took on his body?

ADEDIGBA: Yes. He swore, he was asleep on the night, I swore he came to the palace to persuade me. Overcome by the powers of his trickery, I attacked Atiba.

AKUDA: Ewo! By the gods! That was why my Ilari gave up his life. No one was to wage a war against the people of Atiba as long as I or my son lived in it. Esu lalu was our witness.

ADEDIGBA: How were we to know? We captured the Balogun of Atiba.

AKUDA: Kabiyesi, no!

ADEDIGBA: Drunk again and urged on by the evil spirit,

I asked for his head.

AKUDA: You should not have done it, son.

ADEDIGBA: How was I to know? How was I to see that the little corner fire would burn down my own hut? How?

AKUDA: No. you should not have lit the fire at all. You killed yourself.

ADEDIGBA: Too late, Mother. It is only now that I understand. *(Pause.)* No wonder.

OLUAWO: What, Kabiyesi?

ADEDIGBA: That day, as they cut his neck, mine was in pain. Every swipe of the blunt cutlass on his neck, left a thread mark on my neck. Round it like a chain, it circled round. See, Yeye. *(Shows* AKUDA.*)* The same marks on the neck … his neck … his bodiless head which haunted me in my dream. The same one which gave me the message of death. I say, see, Yeye.

AKUDA: Ha … that is it, then … Death wants you. The strange woman wants you. In killing your twin brother, you snapped the sacred cord that binds twins together. You tore everything, child. Everything!

ADEDIGBA: How can you help me, Yeye? I don't want to die. I don't want to join him. I have no child to bear my name. No heir to sit on the throne after I am gone. Help me, Grandmother.

AKUDA: *(Chuckles.)* You say you saw your cut-off head

56

speak with you?

ADEDIGBA: Yes. But I swear I did not say a word to it in my dream. I swear, Yeye.

AKUDA: *(Chuckles.)* Did you have to say a word to death? Was the calabash not already broken and the water not already poured? *(Slowly, she unwraps the osugbo tied around her waist.)* Here, a glorious gift for a king. Take. This may help you.

OLUAWO: No! Kabiyesi. No! Remember Saura's warning.

ADEDIGBA: Oluawo, has Saura not done enough harm? Haa … Yeye, I am grateful. *(Hesitant.)*

AKUDA: Take it from me, son. Tie it round your waist. It may ease your passage. And now, your promise of helping me sleep easier.

ADEDIGBA: Done. A befitting burial fit for a Queen shall be given to you today. I swear.

OLUAWO: Kabiyesi! No!

ADEDIGBA: Hush, Oluawo! It is only a promise for a gift from my grandmother. *(He takes the osugbo. Ties it round his waist.)*

AKUDA: Now, your life is welcome. I smell it already But do not rush to bury me just yet. The spirit of the strange woman still looms. I think she let me die by my cursed son, because I separated you and your brother. When all these are forgiven and forgotten, build me a befitting shrine by the well. But let my body remain there. The cool freshness of the water keeps the tan of my skin. Do not worry, we shall meet very soon. Now go, son! *(As she turns her back to them, slowly lights go off.)*

OBA ADEDIGBA'S *palace.* IFAJANA *sits with him.* OLUAWO, JAGUNA *and* OTUN *are present.*

ADEDIGBA: I was asked to climb the highest mountain, I climbed it and jumped off at the peak. They said I should swim the longest river, I swam the widest and longest ocean, but my plight remains. My severed head pronounced my own death. Everywhere I have gone, I got only clues from those who offered to help. But clues are not the solutions to problems. I must not die. The lives of expectant mothers remain in jeopardy. Strange illnesses claim innocent lives, and I remain helpless. Why would my own head announce my death in the sacred room where the kings are buried? Why?

OLUAWO: If the Oba is not happy, the village cannot be happy. Another reason for these ill omens, my lord.

JAGUNA: If the Oba dies, especially now that there is only one ruling house, and no heir has yet been born, the Oba's lineage ends.

ADEDIGBA: You see me, Ifalaja? You see why I hop about like the frog in broad daylight? I have a thousand reasons to hop. But for now, I hop aimless, blind and destined as my head told me, to hop into the gaping jaws of a crocodile, to die!

OTUN: Talk to Ifa, wise one. This king is good; that is why the villagers have not given him up for sacrifice. What does Ifa say?

IFAJANA: *(Consults the oracle.)* In twos I shall find myself. Ogale gale, the horse rider gallops. In two, I shall announce myself. *(Looks up.)* Jaguna!

JAGUNA: Yes.

IFAJANA: When the Oba chose his calabash of name, how many kolanuts did you find in the covered calabash that he chose?

JAGUNA: It was a marvel. Such a mistake had not happened before. In the Igba, the one containing twenty kolanuts which he chose, we found only two.

IFAJANA: Umm. So you should have called him Adedeji according to the calabash which he chose?

JAGUNA: Yes. But that would have also meant that he was a twin ... a taboo in the palace ... the Abore would have been invited to cut off his head at the shrine of Ogun ... and besides, we all could swear he was not a twin ... we blamed the mistake on the new woman who helped us to wash the kolanuts. On our own, we named him Oba Adedigba which was the calabash he would have chosen.

IFAJANA: *(Returns to the oracle.)* Who holds the key to the heart of man? Obirin, favoured and blessed by the grace of Olodumare. Women hold the key to the heart of man. Kabiyesi, who is Olori Mojisola?

ADEDIGBA: My wife. Should I call her? Does she have a hand in this matter?

IFAJANA: No, Kabiyesi. I see her. She is pregnant?

ADEDIGBA: Yes. Will anything happen to her? The future of my lineage lives in her womb. Is she well?

IFAJANA: Yes, I see the solution of our problem lies with her.

ADEDIGBA: Haa, no! Not my child! Not my son!

OLUAWO: Kabiyesi, please.

IFAJANA: I see you are a very powerful king. Nothing frightens you.

ADEDIGBA: Yes … Baba … except dying. I don't want to die. I don't want my son to die, either. Can you help me?

IFAJANA: No, Kabiyesi!

ADEDIGBA: Oluawo, then why is he before me?

OLUAWO: Give me a chance, Kabiyesi. We heard he is good and truthful. We have told him nothing. Let us see how he meanders the curves of the great river without getting drowned. Patience, Kabiyesi!

ADEDIGBA: Alright then, drown yourself, old man, we are all ears. Speak …

IFAJANA: Your father … Your Highness. Ifa says he caused all the problems that you have.

ADEDIGBA: Do you hear this old man and his wrong accusations? My father never had a hand here. No one has mentioned him. Let the poor man rest in peace. My cut-off head announced my death in my dream, not my father.

IFAJANA: Bad omen, Kabiyesi.

ADEDIGBA: Olodumare be praised. That is all we have asked you to find out. Why do I waste my time with you? You have already said that you cannot help me avert my impending death.

IFAJANA: *(Looks up.)* But Ifa insists, Kabiyesi, it is your father we should ask. Let me show you. *(He brings out a white sheet of cloth. Two mesengers hold the edges of the cloth. He throws the opele.)* It is the secret of the past that reveals the action of the future. My fathers, do not shame me. When we wash the eyes of a child he sees clearer. See, Kabiyesi. See! There. Haa ... there!

*(Slowly, lights dim on them. Lights come on the other side of the stage to show the shrine of Orisa Ibeji.)*

ADEBIMPE: Yeye, I am happy you received us.

IYA OLORISA: Orisa Ibeji welcomes you, Kabiyesi.

ADEBIMPE: This is my wife, Olori Titubi, and my mother-in-law, Yeye Akuda.

IYA OLORISA: The great woman from Atiba. Orisa Ibeji welcomes you, too.

AKUDA: I greet the great Orisa Ibeji. The one who gives only in twos. The one whose favour strives in double. The one with the blessings of a thousand smiles. Yeye Ibeji, here, a little gift from us to you. *(She gives her a bundle, which* IYA OLORISA *collects.)*

IYA OLORISA: I am grateful. But what do you want from Orisa Ibeji?

ADEBIMPE: A favour, Yeye. A small favour from Orisa Ibeji for the royal household.

IYA OLORISA: I do not understand.

ADEBIMPE: Forgive me, Yeye. I am the King of this great land of Ibeko. I have twenty-five daughters as I speak. Not one son. Not an heir. Not an Aremo to inherit my throne. No one to sit on my throne after I have joined my ancestors.

IYA OLORISA: I hear you.

ADEBIMPE: My new wife, Olori Titubi, is pregnant, and when we consulted Yeye Osun, she said that Olori carries my twenty-sixth daughter. What kind of a curse is this? Who did I offend? Why would I be blessed so negatively with children who will only adorn my throne, and not lift it up to a higher plain like a son? Why?

IYA OLORISA: So what do you want from me? From us?

ADEBIMPE: I want you to change my female unborn child to a male. I will give anything to thank Orisa Ibeji.

YEYE: A difficult task. Esu Odara must have a hand in this to effect the change. You want us to alter the natural order. To amend the will of Olodumare. Kabiyesi, let this be. Let your wife have the child as Olodumare has given her to deliver.

ADEBIMPE: Ewo!

TITUBI: Yeye, I have gone this far. I cannot turn back now. If Esu Odara wants my head after I have sighted my son, he can have it. If he wants my heart even, he can pull it out of me. I pledge my life to make Kabiyesi happy and fulfilled. He has shown me kindness; I must be the wife who gives him his heart's desire. Do it for us, Yeye.

ADEBIMPE: Great woman, I thank you.

YEYE: *(Chuckles.)* Oba Adebimpe, ekeji Orisa. To ba la se. I shall not pound your yam small, neither shall I cut your morsel small. We shall do it. You will leave Olori and her mother here. The work will be done tonight. I shall need a he-goat to use and some money to get the things we need for the work.

*(Lights go off slowly. Lights come back on in* ADEDIGBA's *palace.)*

IFAJANA: Your father sent a cow. Double of everything Orisa Ibeji requested for. Happy with him, Orisa Ibeji blessed your mother's womb with a set of twins. But the Orisa had said that the twins were never to be separated. So when Akuda … Who is Akuda?

ADEDIGBA: My grandmother.

IFAJANA: She separated the twins.

ADEDIGBA: I know.

IFAJANA: Orisa Ibeji punished her with a slow death. She must not be buried.

ADEDIGBA: Haaa!

IFAJANA: She will return soon. When she does, return her to the shrine of Orisa Ibeji, where she will grow to serve her as an acolyte.

ADEDIGBA: My life, how do I get it back? Like my late father, I have no heir. I want one. I must see my son.

IFAJANA: You will. When your son is born, your life will be returned to you. Your son who is your brother, Taiye lolu ijo l'owo ejire ijo l'oro'le, shall return soon to claim his own. And Orisa Ibeji must be honoured the day after. A basket full of sweet things ... all the things the mouth eats. All in praise of the glory of the gifts of a great goddess ... gifts of Olodumare! Haaa ... even as we speak, Orisa Ibeji smiles on your fortune, Kabiyesi. Soon, another set of gifts arrive for you ... soon, Kabiyesi.

IYA: *(A woman in black aso oke comes in. She kneels, saying nothing. She sobs quietly. All the other chiefs except* OLUAWO *leave the throne room.* IFAJANA *begins to pack his load when* ADEDIGBA *gestures to him to stop.)* Can I speak now?

ADEDIGBA: Yes, midwife of the palace. Your face frightens me. Yet what eyes have not seen this before is to put fear in the heart of the owner of the matter. What is the matter? What have you seen? Speak, woman.

OLUAWO: Is it fish or the crab?

IYA: Fish, my lord. A big fat forbidden fish.

ADEDIGBA: Speak, woman. My ears burn. They stretch to receive the news of my wife's child delivery. First, is she alive?

IYA: Barely. She stands at the crossroads between life and death. She too asks after you. *(ADEDIGBA tries to rise.)* No, Kabiyesi!

IFAJANA: No, Kabiyesi. You must not see them just yet. Here, Oluawo, the ring of life, hurry to her. Put it on her. Put it on the third finger of her left hand. Hurry. Not a drop of water. *(OLUAWO takes the ring and exits.)*

ADEDIGBA: Woman, continue.

IYA: Olori Mojisola had a set of twins.

ADEDIGBA: Haa, ewo! Not me! Why?

IFAJANA: Why not you, Kabiyesi? The rift between you and Orisa Ibeji is now over! With the birth of the twins the process of healing has started. Now she begins to forgive you. Tell Kabiyesi more about what happened, Iya. Speak, woman. Hurry!

IYA: There is one of the twins, the son, he is loud and noisy. His tear drops, thick and salty. His limbs tired as if he had to struggle to return to this world. He would not keep quiet until he snuggled at his mother's breast.

ADEDIGBA: And the female?

IYA: Quiet and mute. She opens her mouth, but instead of tears comes yawns. Her eyes permanently shut. Both when placed together, a beautiful sight to behold. As it is with the custom, Abore is supposed to behead them, one after the other at the shrine of Ogun.

ADEDIGBA: Never! Not my children. Never, woman!

IYA: But our ancestors said ... I have even summoned the Abore. All I need is your nod. Please give it.

ADEDIGBA: *(Angry.)* May the gods blind whoever lays a hand on my children ... Bring them to me.

IYA: *(Hurries out.)*

OLUAWO: *(Enters.)* She is steady now. The ring worked magic. Her breath is normal now. She has returned to us. Ifajana, great one, Kabiyesi thanks you.

*(IYA enters with the two children in each hand. ADEDIGBA takes them. IYA rises.)*

ADEDIGBA: By the powers bestowed upon me by our forefathers, I, Oba Adedigba, son of Oba Adebimpe, hereby revoke the law which forbids the birth of twins in the palace. From this day onward, they remain welcome owners of the palace. Orisa Ibeji is also now a blessed goddess of our land, Ibeko. Every year, we shall worship her, starting from today. Iya they look so identical, I cannot differentiate which one is the female.

IYA: *(Picks one.)* The one with you is the female. She is Kehinde ...

ADEDIGBA: Kehinde Akuda, Yeye dada, you returned. Welcome, our secret shall remain with me. Here. *(Collects* AKUDA's *osugbo from* OLUAWO, *and wraps*

67

*the baby with it.)* There, I return it with gratitude. I return you to where you belong. Take her to the shrine of Orisa Ibeji, where she will serve her till the end of her life. And now, my son. *(IYA gives him the second baby.)* Is this my son?

IYA: Yes, Kabiyesi. The Sooko.

ADEDIGBA: Give him to me. Let me announce him to the world. Let me crown him before his time arrives. To those who thought that as a snake  crawls past a rock, I shall leave no mark, I shame them.

*(Steps out to the  audience.)*

Shame, I mock you all!
Jeers, I stamp on you all.
This is Omo Oba Adewale.
The one called by the spirits to sit on the throne of his forefathers, whom people rumoured will be a figment of my imagination. This is Oba Adewale, the Kabiyesi who has travelled from far and wide through  the high heavens, to the land of Atiba to rule the people of Ibeko who people denied his coming.
*(With pride.)* This is my son.
Mothers of the night, I thank you. Orunmila, Esu Odara, Ogun Onire, Shango Olukoso, gods of the land, I greet you all, men, women, children, I thank you all. Today, I shed the garb of a barren male king … I shed the description of the desperate king in search of a seed
And now I adorn the cloak of a father,
Of a king who begets a king.

Me, Oba Adedeji Adedigba,
Father of Oba Adedeji Adewale.

*(The royal drummers line behind him, and beat out the royal salute as he raises the child. All others greet in unison)*

*"Kabiyesi."*

> *(Lights slowly come to a final fade.)*

*The shrine of* ORISA IBEJI. IYA OLORISA *stands before the shrine.*

IYA OLORISA: My goddess has won. Let it be. The people of Ibeko have realized your greatness, great one … let it be! Today, both the King and Queen have come to give thanks … to pay homage … I say sheathe your mighty sword, great woman.

We shall celebrate you today,
We shall sing for you today.
Haa … here comes the Queen.

*(Enter the* QUEEN, *richly dressed. She carries her son behind her. She carries her daughter in her arms. Four women follow carrying four big plates of gifts covered with white wrappers as they dance in, singing.)*

Ejire ki jo
O loro
Kii jo
Tayelolu
Ki jo loro
kijo

*(The women kneel before the shrine.)*

OLORI: Orisa Ibeji, I greet you. Iya Olorisa, I greet you. These are my gifts of gratitude.

IYA OLORISA: *(As she uncovers the wrapper of the gifts.)* Yes, Orisa Ibeji, they are all here. What you eat. What makes you happy.

Sweet things. Aadun, akara, oka wowo, ireke, epo and ewa elepo. Accept these gifts and give the people of Ibeko children.

ALL: Ase!

IYA OLORISA: Give them wealth.

ALL: Ase!

IYA OLORISA: Give them health.

ALL: Ase!

IYA OLORISA: I shall celebrate this festival with the goddess of twins. Be favourable, Orisa Ibeji. Be favourable to the people of Ibeko. Let this celebration be the renewal of many to come. Come back home to Ibeko and live with them. Come, Yeye. *(MADWOMAN walks in. The maidens try to chase her away.)* No, all are welcome today. Give her a wrapper to cover her up. And a stool to sit. *(To MADWOMAN.)* Welcome, woman, sit and watch. Here. *(She puts some food in a plate and gives it to her. THE MADWOMAN is made to sit close to the two carved twin effigies in the shrine. The maidens wrap a dress round her as she sits on the carved stool to eat and enjoy the performance. OBA ADEDIGBA dances in with his royal horse whisk in one hand, and a male effigy in the other. The other male and female dancers carry effigies, too, singing and dancing.)*

Taye lolu
Nmeye lo o, eyin le seye
Kehinde n me ye lo oo
Eyin le

seye

*(As the dance continues,* MADWOMAN *carries the two effigies, she climbs the stool, taking the posture of the goddess Orisa Ibeji, holding the two effigies in each hand. Lights slowly come to darkness amidst dancing and singing leaving a spotlight on Orisa Ibeji's face for a while as* IYA OLORISA *chants her oriki.)*

Ejire ara isokun
Edunjobi aromose
Oninu ire lo n bi edun omo
Won ni ki edun san wo ile o ko
O ni kaka ki oun san owo ile,
O un a san origin
Edun gbori igi reterete
O be kiti be kese
O be wole alakisa
O so do ni gba aso

*(Final darkness on stage.)*

**The End.**

# Kraftgriots

*Also in the series* (DRAMA) *(continued)*

Alex Roy-Omoni: *The Ugly Ones* (2011)
Osita Ezenwanebe: *Adaugo* (2011)
Osita Ezenwanebe: *Daring Destiny* (2011)
Ahmed Yerima: *No Pennies for Mama* (2011)
Ahmed Yerima: *Mu'adhin's Call* (2011)
Barclays Ayakoroma: *A Chance to Survive and Other Plays* (2011)
Barclays Ayakoroma: *Castles in the Air* (2011)
Arnold Udoka: *Akon* (2011)
Arnold Udoka: *Still Another Night* (2011)
Sunnie Ododo: *Hard Choice* (2011)
Sam Ukala: *Akpakaland and Other Plays* (2011)
Greg Mbajiorgu: *Wake Up Everyone!* (2011)
Ahmed Yerima: *Three Plays* (2011)
Ahmed Yerima: *Igatibi* (2012)
Esanmabeke Opuofeni: *Song of the Gods* (2012)
Karo Okokoh: *Teardrops of the Gods* (2012)
Esanmabeke Opuofeni: *The Burning House* (2012)
Dan Omatsola: *Olukume* (2012)
Alex Roy-Omoni: *Morontonu* (2012)
Dauda Enna: *Banquet of Treachery* (2012)
Chinyere G. Okafor: *New Toyi-Toyi* (2012)
Greg Mbajiorgu: *The Prime Minister's Son* (2012)
Karo Okokoh: *Sunset So Soon* (2012)
Sunnie Ododo: *Two Liberetti: To Return from the Void & Vanishing Vapour* (2012)
Gabriel B. Egbe: *Emani* (2013)
Isiaka Aliagan: *Oba Mama* (2013)
Shehu Sani: *When Clerics Kill* (2013)
Ahmed Yerima: *Tafida & Other Plays* (2013)
Osita Ezenwanebe: *Shadows on Arrival* (2013)
Praise C. Daniel-Inim: *Married But Single and Other plays* (2013)
Bosede Ademilua-Afolayan: *Look Back in Gratitude* (2013)
Greg Mbajiorgu: *Beyond the Golden Prize* (2013)
Ahmed Yerima: *Heart of Stone* (2013)
Julie Okoh: *Marriage Coup* (2013)
Praise C. Daniel-Inim: *Deacon Dick* (2013)
Wale Odebade: *Ariyowanye (The Uneasy Head)* (2013)
Soji Cole: *Maybe Tomorrow* (2013)
Wunmi Raji: *Another Life* (2013)
Sam Ukala: *Iredi War: A Folkscript* (2014)
Bashiru Akande Lasisi: *The First Fight* (2014)
Angus Chukwuka: *The Wedding* (2014)
Prince Ib' Oriaku: *Legend of the Kings* (2014)
Denja Abdullahi: *Death and the King's Grey Hair & Other Plays* (2014)
Walse Tyoden: *Hunting Sekyen* (2014)